Guitar for Beginners

A Practical Guide To Teaching Yourself To Play Guitar In A Week Or Less Even If You've Never Seen (Or Heard) A Guitar Before In Your Life

James Haywire

copyright © 2020

All rights reserved. No part of this publication may be reproduced, distributed, or transmitted in any form or by any means, including photocopying, recording, or other electronic or mechanical methods, without the prior written permission of the publisher, except in the case of brief quotations embodied in critical reviews and certain other noncommercial uses permitted by copyright law.

Contents

Introduction	1
Chapter 1 - Buying Guide for Guitars	3
Chapter 2 - Maintenance for Your New Addition	8
Chapter 3 – How to Read Musical Information the Right Way	11
Chapter 4 – The Only 7 Chords You Need to Know	17
Chapter 5 – How to Transition Chords & Some Other Fun Chords	21
Chapter 6 – Prepping to Play A Full Song	29
Chapter 7 – Practice Makes Perfect: Scheduling Out Your Time	35
Chapter 8 – Fixing Beginner Problems	44
Chapter 9 – How to Move from A Beginner to An Intermediate Guitar Player	47
Chapter 10 – Added Help with Videos & Extra Resources	48
Conclusion	49
Resources Page	50

Introduction

Doing anything new for the first time can be an overwhelming experience. When it comes to starting the guitar for the very first time, there is no difference. You will not know how to use it. In turn, you will have to find ways to learn as quickly and effectively as possible. This may seem like a problem when you do not know how to play your favorite songs, but there is a solution to this problem.

When it comes to beginner guitar playing, the solution is reading this book to uncover all the tips and tricks a newbie should know with the instrument. With these basics in mind, you will be on your way in no time at all. However, you might be wondering why I would have credibility in this area. Well, let me introduce myself. I have been working in the realm of guitars for over a decade and have had the pleasure of taking in all that music offers for the last 30 years. Currently, I manage a team of over 60 musicians every week, as I train, teach, and build up their skills and talents. Though I work with a variety of musicians from vocals, bass, keys, drums, and violin, my time with an acoustic and electric guitar is extensive. I use the same strategies and teaching methods with them, as I will with you in this book.

There are many reasons why you should learn the guitar. But, briefly, here are some of the most important aims you should get your hands on with a guitar. First off, playing guitar is a fun way to pass the time. It is an instrument you can play on your own or with other people. The memories you can make with this instrument are ones that will last a lifetime. Secondly, when you have fun, you will get better quicker than you ever thought possible. There is proof in the pudding that when you have fun with something, you learn it a whole lot quicker. Lastly, learning guitar can open up a variety of other instrument possibilities from the piano to the cello. The opportunities are truly endless.

As it pertains to guitar, each human learns in his or her own unique way. However, some things are consistent across the board. Consistency is the first peg on the board that allows you to learn guitar quickly. When you are consistently practicing through the week, you will see a change in your guitar playing for the better. Next, repetition is another staple of learning guitar the best way possible. When you use repetition to guide your guitar playing, you will learn songs, techniques, and chords quicker and more effectively. Lastly, you should think about simplification when learning how to play the guitar. There are a plethora of chords that a guitarist can learn in the beginning. However, things like bar chords and power chords make a guitar that much more challenging. By simplifying chords, you will not get stressed out by challenging chords. Rather, you will bask in the work that is playing guitar wherever you find yourself.

I can assure you if you read this book all the way through, you will be able to take in the basics of guitar playing in a week. Then, you will surely be able to play your very first song in only 7 days. If you put your head to the grindstone, you will surprise yourself when it comes to learning guitar. This is not a gimmick or a fallacy. You can learn a song that sounds like the real thing. So, do not fret, and get started right away!

Many people get stuck in the mud about playing an instrument like the guitar because they grind through months and months of theory and other aspects of music that are neither fun nor effective at the beginning of the process. With this in mind, the time is now for you to hop on the bandwagon. This method is proven to work because you get to leap into music and songs that you want to play. What a concept huh? As a beginner-friendly tool, this methodology will get you playing your song as soon as humanly possible.

Now that you have a taste, it is time to jump into the world of playing guitar as a beginner. The next 7 days will be life-changing for you, as you embark in the world of music. So, let us turn the page and see what is next when learning the guitar.

Chapter 1 - Buying Guide for Guitars

As we start the first chapter, it is important to know about guitars before you get into the process. Before you can get to learning chords, the string letters, and how to hold your beloved guitar, you have to start with owning one. There are 3 different kinds of guitars and here they are:

1. Bass Guitar: A bass guitar normally has 4 strings, but can have up to 5 or 6 as well. Compared to an electric and acoustic guitar, basses usually have fewer strings. Even though acoustic and electric guitars are used to getting the leading roles on stage, the bass guitar is imperative in a band setting. Especially when partnering with a drummer, a bass and drummer need to be succinct or the whole show can completely fall apart. Think of the bass as the atmosphere or background of the music.

2. Acoustic Guitar: When people think "guitars," the acoustic is probably the most common type for a few reasons. You do not need to haul around an amplifier as you do with bass or electric guitar. There are electric acoustic guitars, but you do not have to worry about that at this point. Even if you do own a bass guitar, they are a lot heavier than the traditional acoustic guitar.  Acoustic guitars are primarily made out of different types of wood, like oak, ash, pine, etc. With a hollowed-out shell, you can attach 6 or 12 strings depending on the sound you are looking for. However, since you are a beginner, stick with the 6 string guitars. You will thank me later. 12-string guitars are a lot more difficult to maneuver than the 6-string type. Acoustic guitars are used specifically in rock, rap, and pop music.

3. Electric Guitar: Many people like an electric guitar because they are loud and proud wherever they roam. Metal is a predominant genre for electric guitars, but you can hear lead electric lines in country, rock, rap, pop, rock, and so much more. It is a well-rounded instrument. Most electric guitars are made with solid bodies, but you can find some semi-hollow bodied electric guitars in the jazz/blues world. With the help of an amplifier, music waves can transmit the sound of vibrations to a heightened level.

For the intentions of playing, as quickly and excellently as possible, I will be focusing on an acoustic guitar, since you can take hold of a bass and electric guitar at a later time. They are perfect types of guitars if you have a general understanding of acoustic guitars. So, by using a 6-string guitar, you will be well on your way to success. But, first, you have to own one.

There are a variety of guitars that you can purchase as a beginner. Some of the more inexpensive models include Yamaha and Breedlove versions. However, if you are looking for an acoustic for the long haul, check out Martin, Taylor, and McPherson brands. These guitars can range from under $100 into the thousands of dollars. As a beginner, it may be smart to start cheaper. However, you may be the kind of person that wants to jump in headfirst. The choice is yours at this stage.

Now that you have an idea about some of the guitars on the market, you need to know the parts of a guitar. Make sure you have a guitar before you start this section, or you may get confused about what is going on. The head is a great place to get this party started, and then we can work our way down the acoustic guitar make-up.

1. Head: If you go to the very top of the guitar, you will find the head. When you see knobs on the acoustic guitar, this is the top of your acoustic guitar. Depending on the type of acoustic guitar that you have, these knobs, or tuners, will be stationed in different areas around your guitar head.

2. Tuners: Every guitar needs tuners or your guitar definitely will not work to its capability. Located on the head of the guitar, these tuners can be manipulated to change the sounds and keys of the string. When you change the pitch of a string, you can rotate the tunning pegs either way for a different sound. You can tell you have a sturdy tuner if it is made out of metal because this version will help your guitar stay in tune longer. Plastic tuners have a very hard time staying in tune though.

3. Nut: When locating the nut, this is the piece between the head of the guitar and everything below it. The nut is used to keep the guitar strings in their place, as you string and tune them to perfection. Primarily, you will see that a nut is black or white. However, you may see some different colors and even ones that glow in the dark, which is a fun thing to think about.

4. Neck: Just like a human neck, the neck of a guitar is one that is right below the nut of your acoustic. On a neck, it holds the head and nut, as well as frets and the fretboard. All parts are important on an acoustic guitar, but the neck can change the sound drastically. This can be for the good or bad, but a lot of times this has to do with the quality of your guitar. Just remember that when you are buying a new acoustic guitar for the very first time, do a quick test for me. Put your hand around the neck. If you can get your entire hand around it, you will have a solid neck. On the other hand, if you cannot get your hand all the way around, you may have some sound problems moving forward with your acoustic guitar.

5. Frets: The metal strips that you see lying on the neck of your acoustic guitar are the frets. You will find them under your guitar strings. Frets help with changing the sounds you are playing on the guitar. This is a good "try me" section where you can test playing the strings. Then, put your fingers on a fret

to play different notes at a time. However, we have got to get to strings first, so hold that thought.

6. Strings: To get sound from a guitar, you need strings. If not and you go up and down a fret, you may get a rhythmic sound, but nothing melodic. The cool thing about strings is you can get sound from strumming, pulling, or hammering on the strings. This will all be terminology we can address later on. When it comes to strings, most are nylon or metal. Nylon strings are a great place to start for beginners because they will be easier on your fingers as they start to callus. Some great string brands include Elixir, Ernie Ball, and D'Addario.

7. Marker Frets: These types of frets do a great job sitting in between your traditional frets. Usually, you will see their markings as circles, but they can have more ornate designs as well. Their main purpose is to tell you what fret you are on, but they can be a style, too.

8. Body: Now, we have come to the body of a guitar. A body's job is to have sounds resonate within it where strings are played. You will notice that some guitars have a whole body, while others have a cut-off. The pros of a whole-body means you get the best sound resonating about. But, on the flip side, you cannot move down as far on the neck of the guitar to play more notes and chords. However, as a beginner, this will not matter as much to you. For a cut-off body, you will lose some sound quality, but you will have more room to play your precious notes.

9. Sound Hole: For the common acoustic guitar, you will see a soundhole in the middle of the body right under where the strings are. The sound has to have a place where the music can come forth. However, with some guitar brands, like a McPherson, their soundhole is not in the middle, but rather near the edge of the guitar. But, no matter where your soundhole is, you will probably lose a pick or two inside that will only come out if you use gravity and start to shake it about. This is not a fun task, but the pick will eventually come out.

10. Waist Line: Did you know that guitars have a waist just like humans? As it pertains to a guitar, this is the area where the guitar's body separates into two pieces. This is the curved area of the body's backside that rests easily on your stomach when standing up or sitting down with your acoustic guitar. This part of the guitar is more for comfort than anything else.

11. Bridge: We are not talking about the game "Bridge" here or talking about crossing a bridge. A guitar's bridge is all about keeping the strings tight. You attach strings into the bridge, but the pins do the job of holding them down for good.

12. Bridge Pins: These pins keep the strings taut, so they stay in tune better. By using bridge pins, you can restring your guitar, but this might be too much of

a chore for a beginner. But, you can be the judge of that in the next chapter. Be careful with bridge pins because they are usually plastic and can break easily if your whits are not about you.

Now that you know the in's and out's of how an acoustic guitar is constructed, it is time to get into the nitty-gritty. So, how do you hold a guitar? I am glad you asked.

When working with an acoustic guitar for the very first time, find a nice, cozy place to sit before you get started. This might be in the living room, by the fire in your den, or on the back porch. Posture is important when getting started, so no slouching allowed. If you start learning bad habits with the guitar at the onset, it will hamper your ability to move forward. Getting injured is not out of the question either. You may not see or feel anything wrong when you play the guitar wrong to begin with, but years down the road, it will come back to bite you where it hurts. Things like Carpal Tunnel are a real problem with guitarists who were not taught correctly or just ignored the warning signs on their own. When you do have your body in the right position, your playing will be smoother. Also, it will be easier to conquer those challenging chord progressions.

Leadoff by sitting with your back upright. Have both feet placed on the floor, and lay the guitar on your leg, so the soundhole is facing away from you. Make sure that your dominant arm is the one playing the strings at the soundhole. Now, this might not always be the case for you (e.g., I am a lefty, but live in a right-handed world, so my dominant hand is up around the neck rather than strumming at the soundhole), but do what is most comfortable for you. To this point, the neck of your acoustic guitar and the floor should be parallel. Do not have the neck angling too high or too low. Your body will not thank you for this.

When positioning your guitar, this should be a simple process. If it takes both your hands to move the neck of your acoustic, you do not have a good position. Just have your dominant hand rest on the body of the guitar, while your non-dominant hand holds the neck (for most people).

Yeah! You got the positioning down. Now, your fingers need to get into place.

Finger Placement & Hand Positioning

The "fretting-hand" is the one that you have placed on the neck of the guitar. We will start here to get your fingers and hands in order. Make sure you begin with your thumb around the back of the guitar neck. The neck will be held between your thumb and your pointer finger. Next, bend your knuckles for your point, middle, ring, and pinky fingers. This will give you more flexibility when looking to play the right chords and notes with your fingers. Your fingertips are the best mechanism to press down strings to get different notes and make a variety of chords. With nylon strings, you will not have to press down very much, but metal will ask more of your finger strength to get the right sound you are looking for. Lastly, do not have multiple fingers touching the same string or you will not get the sound you want at all.

Strumming Positioning

For strumming, have your other hand rest at the top part of the guitar's body near your chest. When strumming, you can move the hand up and down at the frontal part of the soundhole. Your arm should be relaxed as you make the most glorious of music. This is now your strumming hand for the rest of your life. How cool!

Learning To Strum

There is a ton of ways to strum in this day and age. Some use a pick and some use just their fingers. You need to find a way that you are comfortable with. However, as a beginner, go with using only your fingers. With the help of your strumming hand, use your index finger and thumb to make up your imaginary pick. Next, bend your middle, ring, and pinky fingers inward. This way, they will not get in the way of strumming. The nail on your index finger creates the best sound, as well as the middle fingernail as well. Just make sure that you use the nail and not the skin at the bottom of your nail. It can get bloody fast with the wrong kind of picking style. As you grow in talent and skill, you can add in a real pick if you prefer.

Learning To Fingerpick

Conversely to strumming, fingerpicking gives you the freedom to play the strings in whatever order you like. Strumming cannot say the same thing. With your strumming hand back in position by the soundhole, use your thumb to play the bass strings, which are the three strings closest to you with the lowest sounds. These strings are called the 4th, 5th, and 6th strings. The remaining higher strings (1st being the highest string and the one on the bottom, as well as the 2nd and 3rd strings moving back up the body) are played with the help of the index finger (3rd string), middle finger (2nd string), and the ring finger (1st string). The pinky, as one of the weakest fingers for guitar, does not need to be used for beginners. However, some more advanced guitarists add the pinky into their repertoire. Lastly, do not use your nails when strumming here. Use the tips of your fingers to make the best fingerpicking sounds.

Chapter 2 - Maintenance for Your New Addition

You now know what makes up a guitar, the difference between fingerpicking and strumming, as well as the types of guitars. What is next? You need to know how to provide maintenance for your guitar. Even after you put 7 full days into your guitar playing, the strings will start to get old, dust will start to collect, and your frets will have slowly started to grind away. It is truly fascinating what playing the guitar does to the guitar itself.

Maybe you did not buy a brand new guitar, but rather a used edition. No problem at all! You just need to know how to take care of your beauty, and tuning is a great place to start. No matter if you have a new or old guitar, your sound will never be perfect. Music is weird like that, but you will be able to get close when tuning the acoustic guitar on your own. As time progresses, so will your tuning, so do not get nervous if this happens to you. The tuners will slowly unwind over time, or you may want to tune to a different kind of tuning when you are more advanced.

Most guitars come with strings already on them, but you will either need to replace or add strings at some point or another. Especially if you are playing your guitar multiple times per week, you will probably need to replace your strings every month or two.

Guitar Stringing

When stringing your very first guitar, you will need these items: new strings, a string winder, a wire cutter, and a damp cloth. You may not need a string winder, as you can wind the tuner on your own. However, you can get the job done quicker with a string winder. Of course, you can go to any music shop for these items or look online.

1. Loosen Strings: If you do not have strings on your guitar currently, skip to #2. But, if you do have older strings on your guitar, loosen the strings manually or with a string winder. By turning the knobs on the guitar, you will notice the strings have more slack than they had when the instrument was in tune. When the strings are completely loose, you will notice that no sound comes from them when you get to strumming.

2. String Cutting: Now, it is time to get out your weapon of choice: the wire cutter. You can cut the strings in pieces, so they are easier to deal with. Make sure you grab the end of the dangling strings, so you do not make a mess all over the floor. A knife can also be used here, but it is more dangerous for a beginner. Alternatively, some guitarists even just go to the bridge and remove each string as one big piece, depending on their comfort level.

3. Removal Time: An electric guitar and bass guitar just need the strings pulled on and they will come right out. But, for an acoustic guitar, this process will

take a little more time. First, start by taking out the bridge pins. A string winder can loosen the tension even more here, or you can use your fingers to maneuver the tuners. Keep unwinding, but be wary that a string my snap round and get you in the hand. Those strings can be wild ones!

4. Knowing Your Strings: After removal of the old strings, it is time to get the new ones on. Open the new strings that you have purchased. Next, divide them by gauge. Gauge is the thickness level of each string. With most brands, they will give you a color system that tells you where to put which string where, but others will just expect that you know which thickness goes where. Go with the "color by numbers" example to help you out best. Either way, the box will walk you through the process. After you have separated the strings, use your damp cloth to wipe the head and the neck down. Dust builds up under your strings very quickly.

5. Winding Up: Once you have the cleaning done and the gauges in order, it is time to thread your strings and start winding them to perfection. Put each string through the tread of the tuner knob. Using your fingers, or the string winder, slowly work your strings tension level. Nothing is worse then re-stringing too fast and breaking your new strings. Then, you will have to go out and buy a whole new set. The thickest gauge, the low E string in traditional tuning (6th string), should be threaded first, making your way down to the lightest gauge, which is the high E (1st string).

6. Finish With A Stretch: When you have them to the ideal tension, stretch them out a little to get them more malleable. This way, they will play better in the long run. If you do not do this, the guitar will be the worst at staying in tune. After they are tuned and stretched to what you want, use your wire cutters to snip off the excess string at the head, so you do not poke an eye out.

Tuning Your Guitar

Before you can start tuning your guitar, you have to know which string is which, when it comes to traditional tuning. From the high to lowest gauge (6th to 1st string), the strings are as follows: E, A, D, G, B, E. This "standard tuning" is what most songs use in the history of the guitar. As you tighten a knob, your pitch will go higher, and visa versa. In this section, we will talk about how to tune with the minimal use of a tuner. A tuner is the best way to get the perfect sound, and it is best for a beginner. But, it is important to know how the process truly works.

E String: The lowest string on the guitar, and the one with the biggest gauge, is the hardest string to tune because you probably will not know what to tune it to. With the help of a tuner or an online tuner, you can get the first note of E and go from there. Apps can also breed success for you at this stage.

A String: When tuning this string, press the 5th fret for the E string. Strum the E string and then the A string. Do they sound the same? Then, you have the first two notes tuned to one another. Yes! The two notes are also tuned to standard tuning, which is a great bonus as well. From this point, you will do pretty much the same thing to see if the other strings are in tune, as well as being in standard tuning.

D String: By having the 5th fret on the A string covered, strum the A and the D strings together and see if they match.

G String: You know the drill. Put your finger on the 5th fret of the D string and strum the D and G strings together. Do they sound the same? Good. If not, you have some tuning to do.

B String: The B string is a little different for tuning, so read carefully. Have your finger on the 4th fret of the G string, and then you can strum the G and B strings together looking for a unison sound.

E (High) String: You are almost there. Can you feel it? Place your finger on the 5th fret of the B string. Strum the B and E strings together for a flawless tuning.

Terrific Tablature

Even if you have never played the guitar in your life, you have probably heard stories about tablature. There are free sites across the Internet where people can create tablature to help others learn a song. Some leave something to be desired, but some tablature is quite good. Check for reviews, ratings, and rankings to find out what is the best tablature around. When it comes to guitar music, tablature is the easiest way to go.

At first glance, tablature may look like musical notes, but there are some unique differences that you should be aware of. First off, tablature is written out from the thinnest strings to the thickest. The top line on tablature is the thinnest string or the high E string (1st string). With the help of numbers, tablature tells you on what fret you need to put a finger on. The numbers go down the head towards the body of the guitar by way of the neck. Because of this, the fret closest to the head is #1 and so on.

Tablature is written like a book that you would read, so go from left to right. When there is more than one number on a line, this means that you need to play these strings simultaneously to get a full sound. Now, you give it a shot and see what tabs are like for you.

Chapter 3 – How to Read Musical Information the Right Way

Moving on from tablature, it is time to upgrade to musical notes. This will be a step up, but you can handle things as a beginner here. For every musician that has ever played guitar or ever will, knowing musical notes is essential for progress. If you want to play a ton of songs, you need to know notes. There is no way around this. Tabs can get you going, but notes help you understand the complexities of songs and even play the music that was not meant for a guitarist. But, with prior knowledge, you too can do this.

Beginning Concepts

Do you know how to read musical notes? Then, you should move on down the chapter to find more info on dynamics, rhythm, and so on. For people who have an understanding of this, it is time for you to go to Chapter 4. But, if this is all fresh like a newborn baby, then let us get to work, shall we? For complete beginners, you need to know about the staff.

Being Conscious Of The Staff

When you look at sheet music, you are bound to see the staff. This is not something you hold, but rather a sign that looks like someone has been brushing up on their cursive writing. At the beginning of every song, you will see the staff and a few numbers that follow. This will help you as a guitarist in knowing the beats of a song and where the notes should be stressed and unstressed. Then, some hash marks (#) speak to the key the song is in.

Note Orders
Memorization and repetition are key to this point in understanding how to read music. Think of it like reading a book. If you do not understand those words in the book, you will not grasp the story. The same can be said with reading music. But, here is a trick you can use to your advantage. There are some acronyms for remembering the notes on the lines of a staff which are E, G, B, D, and F moving from bottom to top. Here are a few acronyms, but make your own as well:

Every Good Boy Does Football
Every Good Boy Does Fine

Make up your own to help you remember this important part of the staff. The acronyms above share that the first line on the bottom of the staff is an E. The remaining lines work their way up the staff to the high F. There can also be other lines that are written in what are called "ledger lines." These can be above or below the traditional staff lines.

Reading Between The Lines

Want another trick for reading the spaces in between the lines? I thought you might. The spaces spell out the word "FACE." The F is the lowest space and then you can work your way up the staff to the highest space that is an E.

Key Signature Knowledge

To know the difference between key signatures, some symbols can guide you along the right path. You will see signs such as a sharp (#), neutral, or a flat symbolized, and you can have them all over your music. If you are struggling to wrap your mind around a key signature, know there are plenty of songs out there that do not need this advanced information. Many people even create simpler versions for beginners to play that sound like the real thing.

Keeping Up With The Time Signatures

Time signatures are very helpful in telling you what amount of beats there are in the measure of a song. A measure is classified as a space with two lines going vertically on the page. A 4/4 time signature means the song is counted as "one, two, three, four," while a 3/4 time signature would be counted "one, two, three."

The Duration Of A Note

When you work to play music the right way, you must have an understanding of how long a note should last. Notes take a break as well. This process helps to tell you how hard you should play on your guitar or how soft. The whole note is the most popular one you will see. This looks like a hollowed-out "O." When a whole note is in a 4/4-

type song, it lasts for 4 counts. On the other hand, if it is a 3/4 song, you guessed it. 3 counts are what you need here.

Do you have a hollowed-out circle with a line shooting upwards? This is a half note in 4/4-time, it is held for 2 counts. With the help of a filled-in circle and a line shooting up, this is a quarter note. It lasts for one complete count. The last type of note is an eighth note. This marking looks like a quarter note, but the note looks like a wing is coming off the side of the note itself. This is counted as a half note.

Rest Sweet Rest

Name	Note	Rest	Length
Whole Note	o	—	4 beats
Half Note	♩	—	2 beats
Quarter Note	♩	𝄽	1 beat
Eighth Note	♪	𝄾	1/2 beat
Sixteenth Note	♬	𝄿	1/4 beat

In music, there are also rests that you need to understand as a beginner. The first rest looks like an upside-down hat. This is a whole rest and lasts for 4 counts if we are in the traditional 4/4 time signature. The right side up hat is a half rest, and it gets 2 beats of rest. Lastly, you should know a quarter rest, which looks like a squiggle on the paper. It lasts for one count. There are other rests, like an eighth rest, sixteenth rest, and more, but at this level, you do not need to worry about that yet.

Knowing the Different Lengths Of Playing

When it comes to playing different lengths on the guitar, you must hit the corresponding notes from your music. However, this might be more difficult than you first thought. First, since the guitar is a stringed instrument, there is the possibility of playing multiple notes all at the same time. This kind of instrument is referred to as an "imprecise instrument." But, to make this work in your favor, there are few things you still need to do to get familiar with the process.

Strumming – The harder you strum, the longer that sound on your guitar will ring out. But, if you have a quarter note on your music, you will only need to hold the sound out for one count and then move onto whatever the music still has to say. So, first off, know that playing harder does not necessarily mean you will be effective on the guitar.

Coming To A Complete Stop – If you are the kind of guitarist that plays hard, it does not necessarily mean you are going to have trouble with the guitar. However, you will have to put in more time to understand your craft. When stopping, you can mute the guitar with your strumming hand to stop the notes or move onto the next note or chord you are supposed to play.

Repetition – Did you know that there is repetition on a score of music? You will see a double line and dots that look like this:

This is the symbol to repeat whatever you started playing at the beginning of the song. There are a ton of songs that use this to not waste paper and make it easier for the musician.

Making Your Dynamics Dynamite

When playing your song, you may see more information on your music to help you play with appropriate volume. Here is the chart that you should follow:

Soft – Piano (p)
Loud – Forte (f)
Very Soft – Pianissimo (pp)
Very, Very Soft – Pianississimo (ppp)

Very Loud – Fortissimo (ff)
Very, Very Loud – Fortississimo (fff)

There are others that you might see as well (e.g., piu (more) and mezzo (moderate), but they are not as common at the beginner level.

Dynamic Changes

If you have taken math, then you have probably seen greater than and less than signs. The > and < markings do a great job of telling you when to bring the dynamics down and when to bring them up. A crescendo is when you build the loudness up (<). A decrescendo is when you progressively bring the volume down.

Knowing Your Strings

As talked about earlier in tabs, some numbers coincide with the strings on your guitar. Think of it as a roadmap to getting you to complete the song. Some sheet music for beginners will even tell you the fingers to place on the string. This will help you along in the right direction.

Getting Your Practice On

Having theory available to you in your memory banks is a big deal. However, you cannot just be a good musician because of that. You need to practice your craft and work hard to reap results. Now, having to work for it, instead of learning by ear, might frustrate you. Some people just have a knack about picking up a song without needing music. However, if you can do both, you will work to be a very successful guitarist. Check out these helpful tips below to get you practicing better than you ever thought possible.

#1 – Pick A Song

The first thing to do is to pick something you will enjoy. It might seem like a no-brainer, but a lot of people pick a song that they have heard others play or think they should play. In reality, choose something you will love to play over and over. Remember repetition now.

#2 – Sit & Study

Even before you get the guitar out, it is time for you to familiarize yourself with the music. As you read the notes, check out the beats, time signature, notes, dynamics, etc. Practice by making the beats through clapping your hands or hitting your hand to your lap.

#3 – Guitar Time

After you have spent the necessary time working with the song's intricacies, you can pull out the guitar. The prep work may take minutes or hours to do. But, if you have worked hard to prepare yourself, then you will be well on your way to rocking it on the guitar.

Chapter 4 – The Only 7 Chords You Need to Know

When you get to this point in your reading, you are about to have a lot of fun. Learning chords is a game-changer when it comes to your guitar. Until you learn chords, you will be hard-pressed to rock the guitar as you have always wanted to. To start, you need to make sure you know the difference between notes and chords.

A chord is more than one, single note. Instead, it is a conglomerate of notes put together to make a certain chord. As it pertains to a guitar, if you are playing a chord of C major, there are three main notes you have to press the strings down for. With the help of the G, E, and C notes, you will strum them together and make a pleasant sound.

As you start to navigate a variety of chords, know that D, C, and G major chords are some of the most common ones to use. For beginners, they are the easiest to play, and a lot of songs use these chords. At this point, it may be good to remind you about tablature. Remember that tablature is presented vertically. This is to help you pretend that the tablature is like the neck of your guitar. The string on the furthermost right side of tablature is the high E string. Then, from there, you can work your way down as normal.

Continuing with tablature, you need to know a few symbols that are important to understand when reading chords. Some of the most common chord symbols include the "O" and "X." When it comes to the O, it means that you play this string in the chord. O stands for "open" in this example, but you do not need to press down on a string to make a sound. On the other hand, the "X" means you skip over the string and do not place a finger on it or play that string. If you are having a difficult time finding an X or an O, look at the top of the chord chart to see them in all their glory. It is time now to hop into how to play the 7 chords.

Before we get started, you need to know there are a variety of major and minor chords for the guitar. Major chords range from A to G, as well as minor chords from the same range. However, some are much different to play than others, so let us embark on the 7 best chords.

C Major Chord

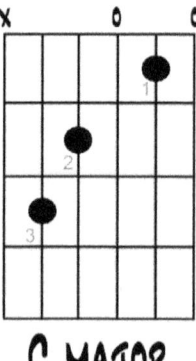

Now that you can read the chord tablature, it is time to start playing. Let us stay in the example of a C major chord, shall we? When reading from right to left, your high E string will be open, your B string will have your 1st finger on the first fret, the G string will be open, the D string will have your 2nd finger on the second fret, the A string

17

will have the 3rd finger on the third fret, and the low E string will not be played with the marking X.

O.K. You have made it through your first chord. Give it a try and get to practicing. The other chords in this key that you should know involve the D major chord, the G major chord, and the E minor chord. They all sound pretty amazing together in a song. Try transitioning through a variety of progressions like G, Em, D, and C, or Em, C, G, D. After a while, you will be well on your way to having some success in the world of guitar chords. But, let us teach you the last few chords, so you can be well-resourced to this point.

D Major Chord

A D major chord is another simple option to play. Starting with the high E string, you need your 2nd finger on the 2nd fret. The B string needs your 3rd finger on the 3rd fret, while the G string needs your 1st finger on the 2nd fret. From there, the D string is open and does not play the low E and A strings. This, in a nutshell, is a D major chord.

E Minor Chord

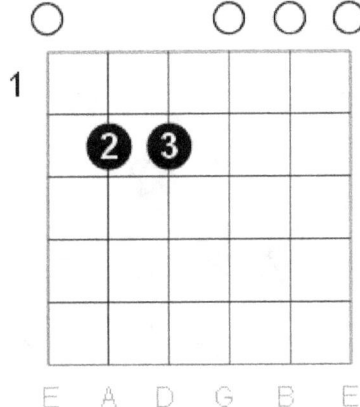

An E minor chord will be the first minor chord you will ever learn. How exciting! Start by playing the high E String, B string, and G string open. The A and D strings need fingers on the 2nd fret with your 1st and 2nd fingers. Lastly, leave the low E string open for a beautifully, sounding chord.

G Major Chord

For the G major chord, this is one of the last chords. You need to play in the key of G major for most songs. As it pertains to this chord, start with your 3rd finger on the 3rd fret of the high E string. Then, leave the B, G, and D strings open, while putting your first finger on the 2nd fret of the A string, with your 2nd finger on the 3rd fret of the low E string. Now, you know 4 chords in the key of G.

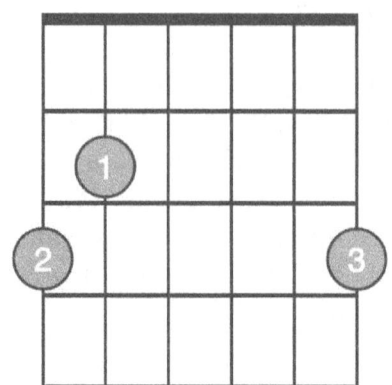

A Minor Chord

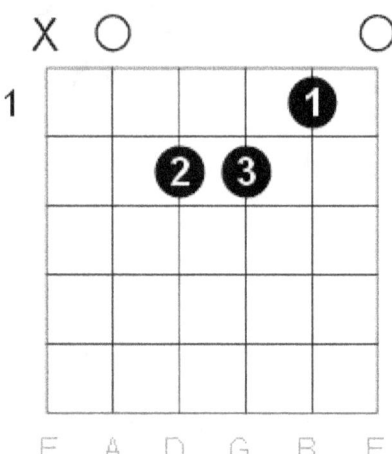

With only 3 more chords to go for beginners, let us get going with another minor chord: The A minor chord. Start with the high E string as open, but for the B string put your 1st finger on the 1st fret. For the G and D strings, your 2nd and 3rd fingers need to be on the 2nd frets. From there, the low E and A strings are open. Then, you will have another ominous minor chord. A minor can be paired nicely with a C major chord.

E Major Chord

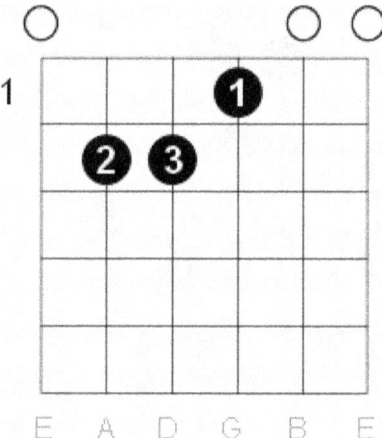

The last two chords are perfect together in a song. Start with the high E string and B string as open. Next, put your 1st finger on the 1st fret of the G string. From there, put your 2nd and 3rd fingers on the 2nd fret strings for A and D, while leaving the low E string open. Now, let us finish with a simplified version of the A major chord to add to your progressions.

A Major Chord

 For our last chord, A major, we are going to do an A2
chord. It is a simple version that you will love when playing your lovely guitar. Start with your high E and B strings open. Next, put your 1st finger on the 2nd fret of the D

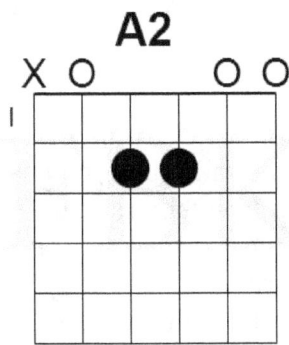

string, with your 2nd finger on the 2nd fret of the G string. Lastly, leave the low E string and A string open for all the world to hear.

You now have a plethora of chords at your fingertips. There are more difficult ways to play each chord, but this is your best way to start. You will not get frustrated and rather enjoy your time on the guitar, as you should to this point in the process.

Chapter 5 – How to Transition Chords & Some Other Fun Chords

You have just embarked in the world of chords, but how do you get from Point A to Point B with your chords? Your fingers have to do the work to make sure you change chords with promptness and efficiency. But, let us get down to business about why you have to practice. First off, chord changing is one of the most difficult things you will ever have to do with a guitar. Even the best guitarists on the planet struggle with this concept, so do not be dismayed wherever you find yourself in the process.

Since you are in good company, you must understand that muscle memory is a big, big deal. Truly, to play any instrument well, you have to have an amazing understanding of chord transitions. This way, you will be well on your way to tying chords together for the best melodies around.

However, at first, you may be a little frustrated with the concept of transition. Even when I started moving between chords my very first time in high school, I, too, was not pleased with the outcome of transitions in my guitar playing. The pauses between the chords I was trying to learn were like the part of the Rea Sea. There was so much space in my chords that the song I was playing did not sound very good. The emptiness of the next note was palpable. However, a small pause is not a big deal. Ultimately, the more you practice and get yourself acquainted with the process, the better you will become. Do not let this process jar you. Your rhythmic timing may be off, but your frustration will soon move to joy when chord transitions start to click for you.

But, how do you do this? So many people chat about how to play guitar, but very few set out tangible steps that will resource a beginning guitarist for the long run. With that in mind, here is some advice that I have been given through the years that has helped me to this point in my life.

Starting Slow

Since this is a very confusing process, feel free to start slow with transitional chord changes. Know that this process will not just come to pass the next day. You will need days, weeks, and months to master guitar concepts. I mean you are a beginner, after all, so cut yourself some slack. Especially with quick songs, you will notice the difficulty in the playing of faster rhythms and trying to move your fingers faster and faster to get the right notes correct. If you practice rhythms too fast, you will start to build up bad habits that you will regret down the road. You will lack a smooth playing style because of your hurried movements. None of us start playing guitar as a professional, so start somewhere and work up to success.

Try playing your song slow, even if it is a faster song. You can work the tempo up and see results from the more time you put in. I wish I could give you more tips and tricks here, but the fact of the matter is this revolves around how much time you are willing to spend practicing the guitar.

If you are busy and only get around to practicing guitar once per week for a short amount of time, you probably will not see much improvement. On the other hand, you may be in a place where you can practice every single day or at least every day for 10-15 minutes. Do not burn yourself out, but rather do the practicing in short bursts to maintain successful practice habits.

Think of playing the guitar like trying to run a marathon for the first time. Most people cannot just hop into a marathon without training. It takes persistence and consistency to build-up to the event. The same can be said for playing transitional chords on the guitar. Playing smoothly is way better than choppy guitar execution at this point in the game.

Also, when you start slow, you will notice yourself relaxing and enjoying guitar like you never thought possible. There are so many parts of the guitar that can go wrong if you are not aware of them. With this in mind, you will notice your movements with the guitar and discover what you do well and what leaves some things to be desired. When you work slowly, you will get better and better because you can fix the problems of your guitar playing while you go.

While you are in a relaxed state, you will not lash out at your guitar. This mainly will be because your mind is in sync with the way you are playing appropriately. The training of your mind and body is essential when it comes to beginning guitar playing.

One Step at A Time

The common cliché of one step at a time may be overused, but it applies perfectly for beginning guitar use. A mistake that is often seen of beginners involves people trying to connect chords over and over to start. Because their focus is shifted from the individual chords, they become sloppy in the way they work on their craft. Never give second-best on the basic elements of the guitar. Everyone says they play guitar, but few know the ins-and-outs of an instrument that is life-changing for many across the globe.

Since your transitions can sound off, people focus on this element rather than the general chords. Be a pro chord player before you even touch transitions. When you have chords down to a science, only then should you move on to the next area of expertise. So, play the chords first and move on second.

One exercise that can help you on the way to glory involves arranging your fingers to make the appropriate chord before you even touch the strings to pluck. By not playing the strings on the guitar, you will notice the muscle memory of putting your fingers on the strings, removing them, and starting all over again before any strumming. After your muscle memory has grown, you will start to have an innate skill that you do not even need to think about in the future.

Next, you can add another chord to the mix. Put your first chord into position and then move to the other chord that you have chosen. With this in mind, do not strum the chords still. This truly will save you from the problems that could haunt you for the rest of your life if you are not careful. And, since you are focusing on the most difficult parts of guitar playing to start, you will reap the benefits down the line.

It is amazing what the human mind can do when you train it right. The neurons and synapses in the brain will be firing in a way that makes a new connection, building the strength and fortitude of your musical knowledge. Even if you are having problems making these connections, there is certainly no reason to worry here. Have a friend, family member, or skilled-guitar acquaintance look at how you are switching between your chords. They can give you some much-needed assistance that will help you nip any problems in the bud.

Lastly, you can use a mirror or record yourself as you mimic playing the chords. This helps because you get instant feedback when seeing if you are playing the chords right, instead of looking down at your hands to see where the problem is. These are some good ways to vary your practicing to help find success.

Limit Easier Chord Versions

I know earlier, I gave a watered-down version of the A major chord. These are great to know because they give you different ways to play the same chord. However, it is in your best interest to get to playing full chords as quickly as possible. Since there are a ton of advanced chords, you may seem overwhelmed with the options you have to choose from. However, find some that are not too hard, but not too easy either. If you pick too easy chords, you will struggle when learning other important chords that are more difficult down the road. On the other hand, if you put your head down into the world of advanced chords, you may give up on the guitar right after you get started.

There is a balance here that is essential for success. However, it is up to you and how you are feeling about the guitar. If you feel like the chords you are working on are too easy and you have mastered them, move on to other more challenging versions. On the other hand, if you find yourself struggling and getting stuck in the mud with a certain chord, then it may be time for you backtrack a little bit to find options that are best for you and the skill level you are a part of. So, in the end, do not be simplistic, but do not think you need to conqueror the world of the guitar right away either.

Metronome Usage

You may get so caught up in the world of chords that you forget rhythm altogether. But, if you have rhythm on your radar, you will learn a lot quicker when dealing with chords. Think about your favorite song in this day and time. How do you feel when you listen to it? Do you dance? Move? Sway? Head nod? Tap your foot? Clap your hands? All of those things involve rhythm. Along with a beautiful melody, the rhythm keeps the song moving forward.

As you work towards mastering a chord, know that there is a rhythm that has to be mastered as well. When rhythms and a melody are in order with one another, you will notice the switching between chords will be a whole lot easier moving forward. The faster the rhythm you are playing, you will start to notice uneven beats going on. But, remember that you need to pace yourself. This way, you can work your way up and not build any bad habits along the way.

Speaking of not creating bad habits, think about using a metronome. What a metronome does is show how quick you need to be playing a certain song. As stated earlier, you can start the rhythm slower and work your way up. Another great thing about a metronome is the fact that you can stay on beat with a metronome instead of going faster and slower during a song. When you stay on and in the groove, you will not feel pressure about the process of mastering a song.

What a metronome does is measure your BPM or "beats per minute." Songs can range in the double digits up to the hundreds. If you are having a hard time keeping up with the last song, what do you think you should do? Well, of course, you should slow everything down and work your way back up the mountain. You never help yourself when you butcher chords. Backtracking will help you in the long haul.

Common Chords

Earlier, I expressed the importance of the value in knowing the G, C, D, and Em chords. There are truly thousands and thousands of songs that are at your disposal whenever you want to get learning something new in the digital age that we live in. Luckily for you, the most common chords you will see in many songs only need G, C, and D chords. By learning and switching these chords successfully, you will be a better guitarist and a better musician, as you get older and wiser. If you are looking to find a lot of free resources for songs you like, check out Ultimate Guitar Tabs.

Passing the Barre

After you have worked through some of the easier chords in the guitar world, it is time to get familiar with the barre system. Barre chords are needed in the guitar world for a few reasons. First off, when learning barres, know that you may have a harder time learning these chords than the other ones your first started with. Of course, do not even play barre chords to start. Just get your fingers to work with traditional chords first and then move onto barre chords.

As it pertains to barre chords, you will have to put your entire 1st finger across a fret and press down. This takes a lot of precision and pressure to get the sounds you want coming out of your guitar. Try to barre your 2nd, 3rd, and 4th fingers, as well, ranging from the middle finger to your pinky. Notice the difficulty certain fingers have with laying down on a fret and giving pressure to the strings to make a sound. If you do not have a barre placed down appropriately, you will have problems where some strings are muted and others are not.

After you have barres down to a science, it will now be time for you to try to do other things with the rest of your fingers. For example, barres have different chord forms that create other sounds. Whenever you play a barre with an E major chord form, you will be able to play a variety of major chords when you move your barre up and down on your frets. On the other hand, if you are looking to play barre minor chords, then you need to play an A minor form more to know a variety of options on the guitar. There are countless ways to play the same chord. You just have to work your way up to figure out what the barre system can do for you.

Having the Power At Your Fingertips

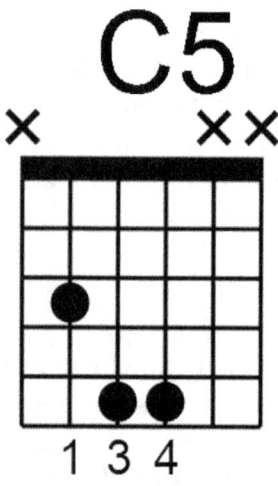

Now that you know the barre system in and out, power chords are next on the list. When it comes to power chords, know that they are made up of two very distinctly different notes on the guitar. To give you an idea, let us use the C5 chord for a reference point. The C5 chord has a root note, as well as a major scale 5th note that you will use.

Power chords, as can be surmised from the name itself, are perfect for metal and rock genres of guitar. Think of bands like Kiss, Journey, Nirvana, Red Hot Chili Peppers, Queen, Green Day, Boston, Michael Jackson, The Beatles, and Chicago, and you will hear power chords all over the place. With the help of one or two fingers, you will have power chords down. When doing power chords, you will be able to play the chords on different octaves and transition smoothly up and down the neck of the guitar, while getting a great baseline sound in the process.

Another thing about power chords is the fact that they are neither major nor minor, so they fit well since they use the root and 5th of a note. Power chords are not the most difficult chords on the planet. But, switching may take some getting used to.

Moving Chords Around

As you move chords up and down the fretboard, whether you are using a barre or power chord, you will get something different out of each one. Let us say you are using a power chord F. If this power chord is moved to the 5th fret, you will get an A power chord, But, move it up two more frets to the 7th fret and you will have a brilliant B power chord.

When you have roots and 5th notes down, you will understand moveable chords in a whole new away. You can move your chords in whatever fashion you are looking for, up and down the guitar's neck. This way, you will own the fretboard of your guitar.

Barre chords are amazing moveable chords as well. Now, do note that barre chords are much more difficult than power chords, but you should try this out for yourself. You probably will not be able to handle barre chords movements at the very beginning. However, remember that if you do not play the chords to start, and get your fingers in the right position, you will gain some amazing muscle memory.

I remember when it was the summer of my senior year, and I wanted to learn "Hey There, Delilah" by the Plain White T's. I was so overwhelmed by tablature and how to play, that I was pretty fearful of the process. But, I stayed up almost all night one summer evening to learn the song. It was the muscle memory over a decade ago that has propelled me where I am today in playing guitar. And I can still play that song today because of muscle memory years ago. But, it was not overnight. I still had to work for weeks to perfect the song before I played it for my girlfriend at the time. Oh, the things you do for love, am I right?

From that experience, I learned a little more than I knew before about the guitar. This has continued to be true years later, as I work to learn a variety of advanced chords to vary my style and usage. Another way to work with moving chords is to play with other friends. Who cares if it is 6 of you playing "Don't Stop Believin'" by Journey together? You can try to match each other's guitar playing to find out how your transitions are and what they are supposed to sound like. Remember others' feedback is important in the process of playing the guitar as a beginner.

As you get better and better on the guitar, know 12 keys can be moved up and down the fretboard when you play guitar. There are some basic shapes that we talked about earlier, like the E and Am form. Other fun barre shapes can make guitar fun as well.

Em Barre Shape

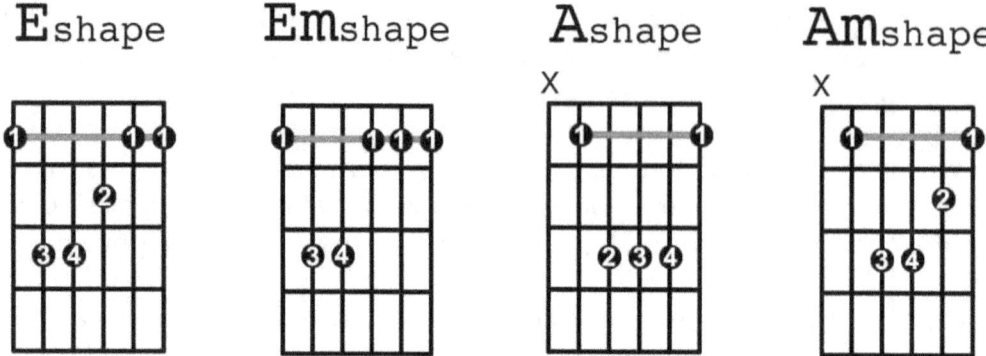

When diving into the basics of a guitar barre chord, E minor is a fun one to consider. With the help of your 1st finger, you can barre a fret and then up your game with the 3rd and 4th fingers on the 3rd fret to get an appropriate barre chord. This is another one of those barre chords that will give off an ere minor sound.

A Major Barre Shape

As a beginner, we will hit one more option for you to analyze. Just remember that there is a whole world out there that needs to be had with guitar barre chords. Remember to use the A major shape, which asks you to barre with your pointer finger, as you place your pinky on the B string 3rd fret, your ring finger on the G string 3rd fret, and your middle finger on the D string 3rd fret.

As you dive into this newfound world, remember that the E major barre chord is probably the easiest one to use. Practice, use repetition and mimic what the chord is like before you even play it. Then, when you have this down, you can press on the strings to see how things sound. If your barre chord sounds good, then you have fully pressurized the notes in the best way possible. However, if you are dealing with some muted sound, you do not have even pressure. Backtrack to find the issue and try, try again. When everything does ring out, it will be music to your ears.

Did We Mention Practice?

You are doing something new for the first time. Are you going to be good at it? Probably not. Things will presumably not go the way you wished. What should you do? Make sure to practice. You will not be able to move forward into the moderate levels of guitar playing if you do not have transitions down. Once your chord transitions do not have a pause in between them, you will be able to handle the toughest songs on the planet.

When you are not thinking about the music, but just handling chord progressions naturally, you will be well on your way to the moderate levels of guitar playing. Start thinking ahead and prepare for the future. When you look ahead at what is next from your song to get to the next level of guitar playing, you will be a real musician at work.

While practicing, make sure that you keep your fingers close to the fretboard. However, do not touch the fretboard. If you do, you may interfere with what your other fingers are doing. A seamless transition is what you are looking for during guitar playing. But, if your hands are ready to roll on your guitar, the possibilities are limitless.

Is it a fast process? No, but to improve your playing, you have to work hard. Most people work up to where they want to get in life. Sure, some might get lucky, or live off the life of previous family members. But, what kind of life would you live if you do not put in the blood, sweat, and tears to be successful? There is nothing more rewarding with a guitar than when you bust your bacon to get to the pinnacle of guitar playing.

Do not give up. Never give up. Frustration may try to take hold, but know that you are a warrior. There is nothing you can't do if you put your mind to it. If you do run into frustrating times with the guitar, give yourself a break and take a break. Pour yourself a drink, and have a snack or two. Even a 10 to a 15-minute window can be very helpful if you are frustrated while playing the guitar. During this time, your muscle memory will start to take hold as well.

Chapter 6 – Prepping to Play A Full Song

You may be painstakingly going through a song at this very moment. But, there are still some ways to help you along. Let us spend some time in the scale world, shall we? When working with music, scales are crucial in your understanding of the inner workings of a guitar. As it pertains to scales, there is a collective of notes that ascend and descend in pitch. To this point, you may be thinking about the need for scales. Here are some reasons you need scales in your life.

#1 – The Dexterity of Fingers: When you work on scales, your fingers will reap the rewards. Your fingers will get nimbler to play chords, power chords, and barre chords. With your dominant hand, it will be easy to see that you can train yourself. Then, as you grow in guitar maturity, you will be able to handle fingerpicking other songs swiftly.

#2 – Getting to Know Your Friendly-Neighborhood Notes: Knowing guitar notes in and out help benefit you. As you play chords traditionally, most people do not necessarily think of the notes. But, with the help of scales, you will be able to consider each note that will help you down the road.

#3 – Understanding Your Music: As you firm up your scales, you will be able to get more creative when you play the guitar. Many guitarists feel like they cannot get creative when it comes to the instrument. However, with the help of scales, you can start to break free from traditional chords and notes, and do things the way you want.

Now, when you heard that we were going to work with scales, you may have had a visceral reaction. Something about musical theory does not jive with many people in the 21st Century. Even though scales are not the most fun things to do, you should still get to work on them. They may not be the most exciting things on the planet, but they are not the dullest things either. Comparatively to chords, scales are blander but think of the knowledge you will gain here.

In the world of instant gratification and getting more stuff, scales might not seem worth it, but I assure you they are worth your precious guitar time. We love to receive things and get positive feedback all the time. However, you might be bad, very bad, when you start scale work. But, have no fear because progress is near if you will only put your mind to it. Scales are not a mindless activity. Think about what you are playing and learn your scales to perfection. The more you practice said scales, the more you will see they are a lot more fun than studying them in a theoretical way.

To this point, some may wonder why we did not start with scales first instead of chords. Well, chords give you something to do when getting started. With this in mind, you get some strumming practice to boot; so, then you can learn what notes you are playing with the help of scales. Whoa! What a concept.

When working on scales, know that they are not separate from chords, but rather connected. After you have gone through major scale work, you will probably come to understand chords even more than you first did. Scales are like the cornerstone of a home or the legs on a table. For every piece of music, you come across, harmonies and melodies will come to life with the help of scales.

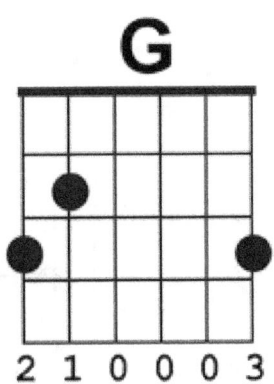

By seeing the entirety of a constructed scale, you will be able to pick out melodies and so much more on your way to mastering the guitar. But, how does a scale work? Let us use the G7 chord as our example to get us started with scales. The G7 chord, in its entirety, comes from the major scale of C. An even more technical term, the "mode," calls this the "G Mixolydian." That is a big word that says that every note in a G7 chord connects with a C major type of scale. How cool, right?

Other types of scales include Ionian, Dorian, Phrygian, Lydian, Aeolian, Locrian, minor pentatonic, major pentatonic, and the blues scale. Know you will not need to handle every single scale to be successful with the guitar to start. But, you should have your head wrapped around the most important scales for the betterment of your guitar career.

Knowing the difference between a major and minor type scale is important as well. You might not fully grasp the concepts at hand, but they do make up the major and minor chords you are learning to play as well. But, as a beginner today, let us just try to focus in on a smaller amount of scales for your sanity, shall we? Some scales get used a lot more, kind of like chords.

To start, get acquainted with a minor pentatonic scale, a natural minor scale, and the blues scale. With these 3 scales, you will be able to hit a lot of genres of music that you are probably interested in playing today. When it comes to the 3 types of scales, know that they are all rooted in the key of A. This means that you can find the root of the note on the 6th string, 5th fret.

Before we continue, some might be lost on what "pentatonic" actually means. A pentatonic type scale is one that has 5 notes in it. For electric guitars, this is where guitarists can have solos and riffs for rock and blues type of music. Speaking of blues music, know that a blues type of scale is probably more a pain in the butt than a pentatonic scale. It is one note that does the damage here. To move into a blues scale from a minor pentatonic, you get to throw in a blues note that everyone around you will enjoy. Ideal for a jazz or blues setting, you get to flatten the 5th tone for added effect. So, if blues is your jam, make this scale top priority in your life.

A natural minor scale is a fun one to obsess over, but do not get so overwhelmed by it that you may quit the guitar altogether. This scale has its place too. However, the challenge level is more extensive. With a natural minor scale, like A minor for example, you will be dealing with 7 different notes. This scale comes from a major scale, but there is a catch. The natural minor scales starts on the 6th degree. With its nickname as the mode of "Aeolian," the natural minor scale is one that delves into pop music. So, once again, if this is your kind of jam, know the natural minor scale in and out.

From here, as stated, there are a plethora of scales for you to observe and take in. But, if you are looking to play a complete song and/or play with a band, check out another famous pentatonic scale, which is called the E minor pentatonic scale. Now, this version is the watered-down edition, but you will get a lot more benefit out of this scale as well. Used in a lot of guitar solos, there is plenty you can be doing with this type of scale.

The Ionian scale might be another scale to spend some time on as well. Also, referred to

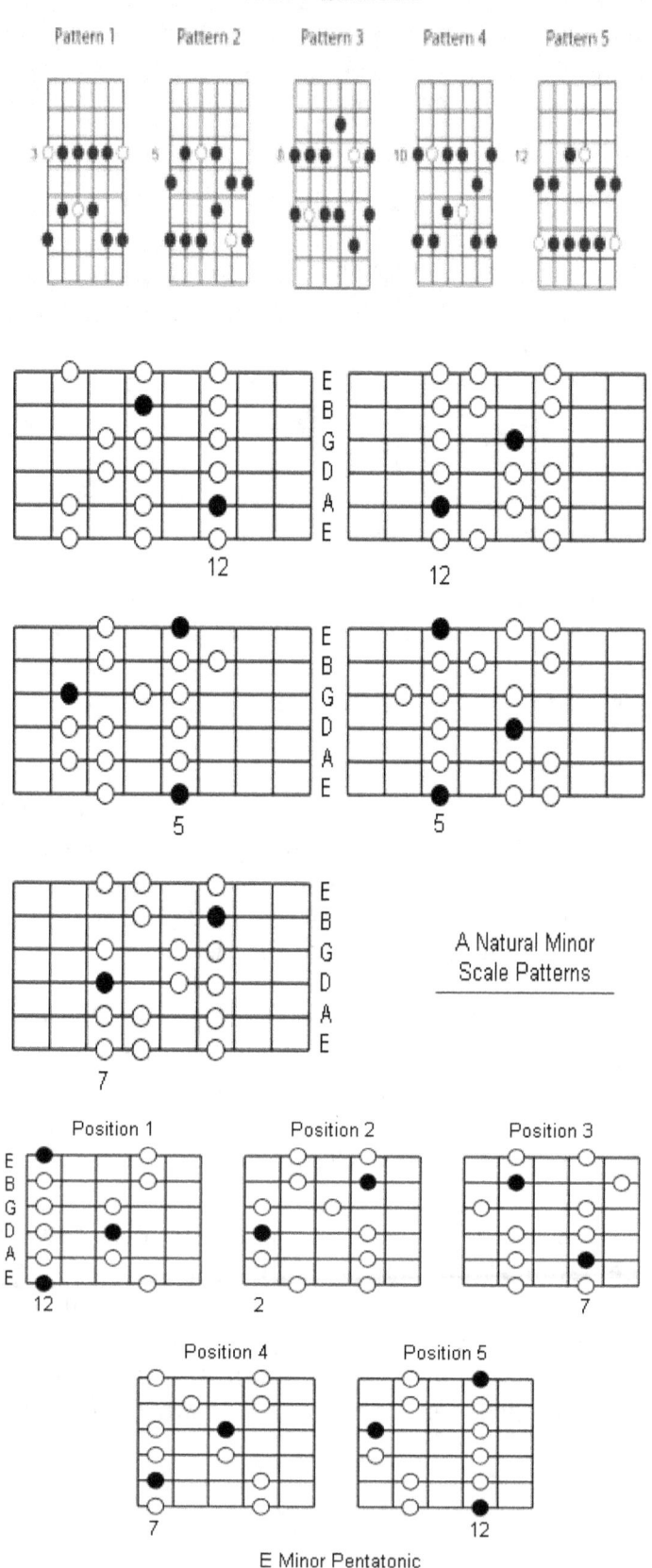

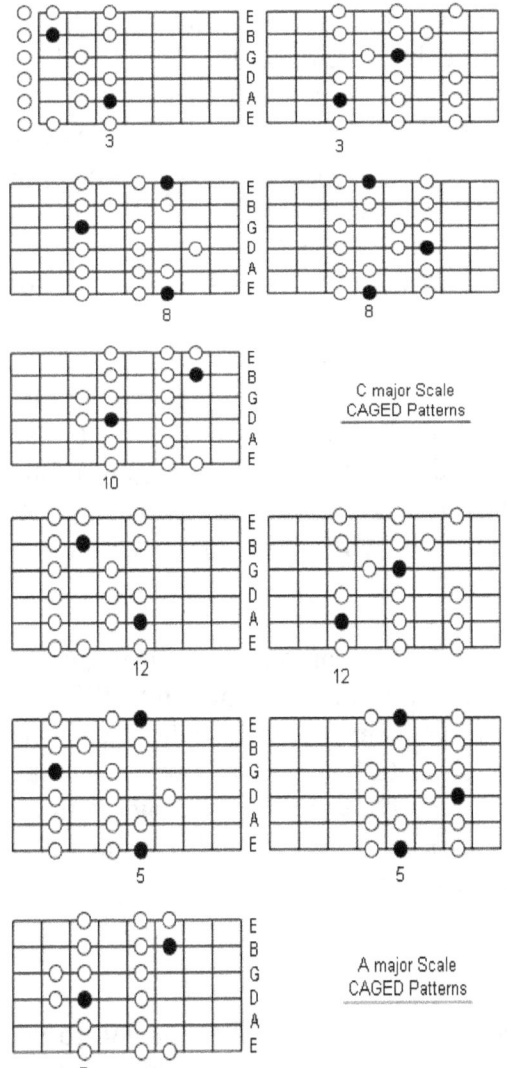

as the "C major scale," this is classified as one of the easiest scales to use in human history. That might seem outrageous, but you can handle this scale as a beginner. With no sharps or flats, your mind does not have to go into confusion to figure things out. With all scales coming from C major, think of this scale as the mother of all scales.

Still, if you are struggling with scales, the pentatonic A major scale should do for you. This scale is a great entry point into the world of scales. Its simplicity is nice and its amount of uses will be enormous over your lifetime of playing guitar. And moving from scales, you have to understand its significance in the world of playing a full song. Not only will you be able to know how to play chords and notes for a song, but you will also know why they are the way they are.

Think of scales in this way. In the subject of math, you may come up with the right answer, but if you did not move towards the answer by showing all your work, do you know the subject matter in and out? As stated, there are more scales in the world, but you have the basics, so run with them. With the help of practice and retention, you will be able to play full songs with ease.

Also, think about imagery to help you on your path to greatness as well with guitar. In your mind's eye, or when you close your eyes, think about where a note is on the staff, or what are the notes for a certain type of scale, or how to play a chord without even strumming them on a guitar. This mental imagery will help you on your way big time. By thinking more about the notes, you will be able to play them quicker and more effectively in the long run.

Well, what if you are struggling with a certain type of scale or song? What should you do? Good question. I am glad you asked. Work on one note of the progression at a time. This kind of focus will help you see where you are falling short. Pull out the handy-dandy metronome again to help you, too. The rhythm portion is key, as stated earlier. Think BPMs here because they will help you with the speed of your playing no matter if you are dealing with scales or chords.

Next, try playing songs or scales by ear before you even take a look at how you should play them. This means that you can think about how the song or scale sounds, and see what you can reproduce. Who knows? You may be able to reproduce a song better than you ever thought possible. But, in the end, you have to decide how serious you are going to be about the guitar. If you can practice 20 minutes per day / 7 days per week, the chords and scales will get easier and easier as you work. But, do not just settle when things start to get easy. Every great musician through history worked harder and harder to be successful in the guitar world, and the same can be said for athletes, artists, and poets.

If your forte is doing solos on a guitar, then you should spend more time with scales. Start with 5 or 6 scales, so you can work your way up to 20. Still, do the 5 or 6 well before you move ahead. Do not be the jack-of-all-trades when you play the guitar. But, if you are going to be a rhythmic guitarist, set your sights on power chords, barre chords, and traditional guitar chords. Knowing all will make you even more dangerous, but you have to start somewhere, right?

Continue using a metronome. You can find a metronome as an app on your phone, at the store as a little machine, or you can use a metronome on the Internet. With the help of a said metronome, work on ascending and descending with scales. Go to the lowest scale tone and up to the highest. Also, if you vocalize the notes while playing them, you will remember the sounds they make. If you cannot do a scale by memory, either print it out on paper or put the scale on your laptop, tablet, phone, or desktop computer. Then, work to memorize scales to the best of your ability.

Getting Your Exercise with The Fretboard

Moving up and down a fretboard needs to become something simple for you to do. Instead of descending and ascending up and down your scales, change directions at random times. For example, if you are doing the C Major scale, start at the note C and begin C, D, E, F, G, and stop at this point. Go back down: F, E, D, and stop. Then, go back up. You can randomly go wherever you want, but you will be hitting notes that matter on this scale.

Do you want more exercises? I am glad you are looking to challenge yourself because this next one is a little more advanced for a beginner. But, you may be able to handle it. For example, you could start with an A minor pentatonic scale. As you end it, move to a C Major scale. You can do this with any scale. Things might sound a little funky. But, overall, you will be furthering your skills like never before. This exercise will be reasonably more challenging, but you will start to see the full picture of the guitar, as we know it.

How about you mix scales together? You can instantly get creative here. Once again, you may get some funky scale structures, but if you know what you are doing, then you will learn scales like nobody before you and nobody after you. Now that we have gotten through these exercises, you will be ready to crush a song for the very first time.

Nursery rhymes are a great place to start when playing your very first song. They help you with scales and their melodies are pretty easy to decipher. You will not need chords to start, but you can add them later as a second part of the equation. Who knows? Maybe you can sing along while you play as well. Then, you will have made it in the world. To break it down, sing a line at a time while playing. If you did well, then move onto the next line of the song. If you struggled, then start at the beginning of the line and try again.

The same can work for guitar solos as well. Pick out a line at a time and see how you do before you even get sheet music. Do use sheet music if you start to fall short, but do not give up easily and cheat yourself out of the learning experience. Even try to sing if you have mastered all those things.

As you get better and better, knowing a full song may give you praise amongst your friends and family. You may even have others in the world start to notice you. Maybe a rock star getting paid is something you could aspire to be. And it all starts with learning a full song for the very first time. When you are in the mode of jamming and/or singing to your favorite song, the world seems to stop for a little. Your time will feel like it is worth something. This is when you start to grasp moving from a good guitar player to a phenomenal one.

Chapter 7 – Practice Makes Perfect: Scheduling Out Your Time

Wow! You have gotten through all the technicalities of the guitar. Now, it is time for you and only you to put things all together. Truly, the best part about the guitar should be your precious practicing time. But, before we move on, think about what you have learned to this point. Remember different guitar parts and what their uses are. Recollect your thoughts about the types of guitars and the differences between electric and acoustic ones. Think about the things that are most important for you and the things you want to improve. A guitar can cater to you if you know what you want. The foundation that you have at this point will bode well for the rest of your life.

With your guitar tuned and ready to go, by hand or with the help of technology, hold your guitar in the way you were taught. Sure, you may feel like I am a nagging parent here. But, this refresher is exactly what you need to get to the top in the world of guitar playing. Knowing the proper ways to hold your guitar will help you from injury and defeat.

Next, think back to the section about changing guitar strings if they break or you need new ones. Also, remember if this is too difficult for you, get a friend or family to help, or just go to a music shop to have them get the job done right. Consider the types of strings you need as well during this process.

Of course, the bulk of this book has been all about reading music and using sheet music and tabs. Reading music is just as important as knowing how to read an equation or a book. When you practice, you will see little successes moment by moment during your journey of playing the guitar.

What else have you learned? There are power chords, barre chords, and general chords to know. We talked about the differences between open and closed strings for a chord progression. Transitioning between chords is a big deal as well. With the help of a metronome, we surmised the importance of staying on beat and rhythm.

Scales were the last things we talked about. Remember? We rolled through major, minor, and pentatonic scales. To this point, you are ready to practice and play. So, let us get into the easiest of guitar songs to help you on your way to victory. The Internet can be your best friend, but we are going to give you some typical songs that most people in the world want to play.

A great place to start is "Knockin' On Heaven's Door" by Guns 'N Roses. This famous band loves to work with a Cadd9 chord. Do not get nervous about the lingo. You soon will be able to rock it like Guns 'N Roses.

Knockin' On Heaven's Door

Words & Music by Bob Dylan

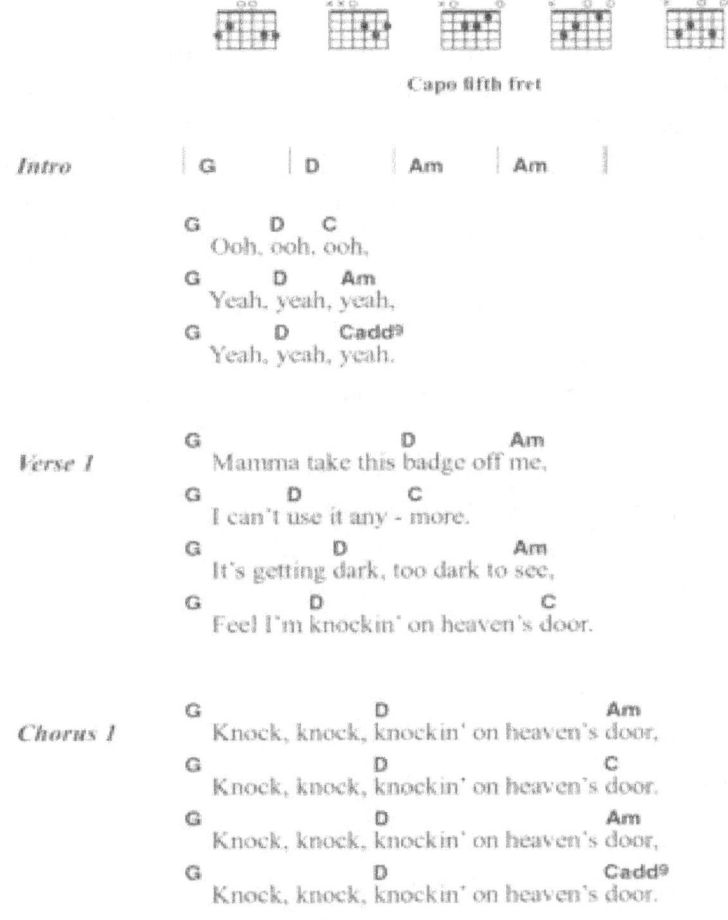

Capo fifth fret

Intro | G | D | Am | Am |

Verse 1

    G   D   C
Ooh, ooh, ooh,
    G   D   Am
Yeah, yeah, yeah,
    G   D   Cadd9
Yeah, yeah, yeah.

    G   D   Am
Mamma take this badge off me,
    G   D   C
I can't use it any - more.
    G   D   Am
It's getting dark, too dark to see,
    G   D   C
Feel I'm knockin' on heaven's door.

Chorus 1

    G   D   Am
Knock, knock, knockin' on heaven's door,
    G   D   C
Knock, knock, knockin' on heaven's door.
    G   D   Am
Knock, knock, knockin' on heaven's door,
    G   D   Cadd9
Knock, knock, knockin' on heaven's door.

© Copyright 1973,1974 Ram's Horn Music, USA.
All Rights Reserved. International Copyright Secured.

For this song, a C major chord can do, but there is a little variance here. For a Cadd9 chord, the high E string is open, the B string needs to be met on the 3rd fret, while the G string is open. For the D string, cover the 2nd fret, and have the A string covered at the 3rd fret. With the low E string not played, you will know how to play the Cadd9 chord to perfection.

You also can learn a Taylor Swift song. There have to be some "Swifty" fans out there in the world still today. The blockbuster song "Shake It Off" is another fun one to play in the world of guitar. Better yet, you only need three chords to be successful, when the Guns 'N Roses song needed 4 chords. For this Swift song, you will need to play A minor, C, and G chords to rock the night away. What is nice with this song is the fact that the entire song goes from Am to C to G over and over again. If you understand that progression, you will not have a problem with this song. Who knows? You may even be able to sing along.

Shake It Off
Words and Music by Taylor Swift, Max Martin and Shellback

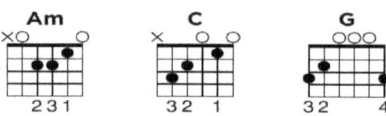

VERSE 1

Fast

     Am   C
I stay out too late, got nothing in my brain.
          G
That's what people say, mm, mm. That's what people say, mm, mm.
     Am   C
I go on too many dates, but I can't make them stay.
            G
At least, that's what people say, mm, mm. That's what people say, mm, mm.

PRE-CHORUS

    Am   C
But I keep cruisin', can't stop, won't stop movin'. It's like I got this
G
music in my mind sayin', "It's gonna be alright."

CHORUS

     Am   C
'Cause the players gonna play, play, play, play, play, and the haters gonna hate, hate, hate, hate, hate.
   G
Baby, I'm just gonna shake, shake, shake, shake, shake. I shake it off. I shake it off.
    Am   C
Heart-breakers gonna break, break, break, break, break, and the fakers gonna fake, fake, fake, fake, fake.
   G
Baby, I'm just gonna shake, shake, shake, shake, shake. I shake it off. I shake it off.

Copyright © 2014 Sony/ATV Music Publishing LLC, Taylor Swift Music and MXM
All Rights on behalf of Sony/ATV Music Publishing LLC and Taylor Swift Music Administered by Sony/ATV Music Publishing LLC.
424 Church Street, Suite 1200, Nashville, TN 37219
All Rights on behalf of MXM Administered Worldwide by Kobalt Songs Music Publishing
International Copyright Secured   All Rights Reserved

While learning these songs, there are a few tricks that you can still have up your sleeves. Start with YouTube to help you on your musical journey. YouTube is a sensational resource that can assert its dominance in your life. You can look up "Shake It Off" and "Knockin' On Heaven's Door." This way, you can play along and see how well you are mimicking the originals.

The next thing you can try is recording yourself. Do not get nervous, but you have to see what you are like when you play the guitar. Also, you can come back to this video from the past and see how much you have improved. You may think that you are playing the song right, but the video will never lie to you about your playing. You can backtrack on a recording to see what mistakes you are dealing with as well.

As you continue to play the guitar more and more, you will notice the constant pressure of your finger pushing the strings down on the fretboard. This will require you to build up callouses on your hands. You might get blisters, but this is a pretty rare occurrence. Your wrists may begin to hurt and the muscles in your hands could start to cramp up. All of these things can happen to a beginner taking on guitar for the very first time.

Also, do not put your thumb over your fretboard. This is known as the "death grip." This grip can cause problems as you try to work towards a natural reach on the guitar. Additionally, it will also be quite difficult for you to move from chord to chord in a song. Your hands will get tired and you will want to just give up. Instead, have your thumb on the backside of the neck. Furthermore, use your fingers to press down the strings.

Of course, we all want to get better but trust the process. Extra haste will not make you a better guitarist. Consistency will make you a better guitarist. With the help of the right-hand positioning, you will nail those notes, no matter what kind of genre you are playing.

You have heard the phrase "speed kills?" It definitely will when it comes to the guitar if you are not careful. You will burn yourself out in the saddest of forms. When you build up the best muscle memory and do not sweat the small stuff, you will get things right in the world of guitar.

The Uberchord Guitar App

If you are looking for another fun way to practice, check out the Uberchord Guitar App. This application is unbelievably amazing. What the app does is listen to you play. That may sound a little creepy, but do not let it weird you out. The benefits of this tool are limitless. As the app listens to you play the guitar, it will tell you when you have made a mistake on a song and focus you to fix the issue. Switching transitions are usually the culprit here.

While working with the help of this app, do not get crazy. Your finger positions and chords were created for a reason. Down the road, you can mess with things to help make the guitar experience more comfortable. However, you should learn the right way first, even if you are in agony at the time (mentally not physically). Relearning chords will not be a fun process for you if you play the chords wrong at the beginning. If you are in physical pain while practicing, stop. Figure out the problem and try to correct it. Do not skip over things. Work hard at the moment to make yourself better. Our world is too transfixed in achieving the goal rather than how they got there. How you get to a goal is most imperative to the success you will have playing guitar down the road.

Practicing Techniques

While spending your time practicing, you should consider some of these techniques to help you on your way. Each technique is in a multitude of songs. So, rest assured you are learning things that will matter in your guitar life.

Muting Life

With this concept, you have the opportunity to mute your guitar. This is a worthwhile skill that involves stopping guitar strings from a resonating sound. Usually, a mute happens at the end of a note to help with transitions. However, this can be a difficult thing to handle. But, you should try it. How this works is using your finger on a note to stop the sound in its tracks. But, putting pressure on the strings will make a noise. Instead, by placing your finger on the note, all sound will cease.

When walking through the muting process, you must understand a few things. First, muting comes in three separate parts. The beginning is probably where you will put your focus. You will find the note you need to play, play the note, and then you will stop thinking about the note. It is a thought process like this that is not great for you as a musician. What you want is to put your focus at the middle and ending part of the note when it comes to muting. When you are playing, this is what people will hear the most anyways.

The middle note is the one that you will want the sound to ring out from, no matter where it is on the fretboard. Then, the end of your note will fade away into the distance. As you work with muting, try to play as smoothly as possible. You want people listening to your music not to notice what goes on at the beginning and ending of your playing. As you blend notes, the last one will fade away, and the new note will take its place. Any choppy notes will stand out negatively. But, when you play genres like metal, choppy is all right depending on the song. Just follow the rules for now, and you can break them as you move from a beginner to a more experienced guitar player.

Muting may not be used a lot in beginner's guitar. But, when muting is needed, know that you will not be perfect right off the bat. This will be a challenging experience to work your way up to robotic perfection. There are a lot of muting techniques that we can discuss later, but for now, let us talk about a few muting strategies.

#1 – Non-Dominant Hand Muting: Whenever you have fretted notes, you can use this muting strategy. As one of the best muting techniques for beginners, you can lift the fingers on the fret off the strings. When you lift the pressure off your notes, the muting will happen instantaneously. However, if you lift your fingers too quickly off the notes, you will deal with excess noise that you do not want. As you practice this technique, make sure that your grip is relaxed. There is a fine line between being too slow and too fast when performing this mute. You are looking for perfection right in the middle here.

#2 – Another Non-Dominant Hand Mute

If you are looking for another way to shorten a note, you can mute the strings with fingers that are not pressing down other strings on the fretboard. Let us say that your ring finger is not in use while playing, but you are looking for a quick mute. You are not necessarily pressing down the strings, nor should you. Instead, touch the strings very lightly with your ring finger.

#3 – The Strumming Hand Mute

Your strumming hand can be a great use when looking for a way to mute as well. Since the thumb is not traditionally used when strumming, this is one of the easiest ways to string mute. On the other hand, if you are using the fingerpicking style, a thumb-mute is a great way to prepare for the next note to play.

#4 – Planting A Mute

If you are interested in using the planting technique, use the fingers from your dominant hand. Once you prepare this ahead of time, it will set you up for success with this muting technique. This might be a technique that you would want to use because it builds confidence in the musician. So, if you are struggling with other muting techniques, why not try this one to build you up. Muting has never been easier with this option.

#5 – Getting Your Ninja on With the Karate Chop

This action might be one of the most well-known in the guitar world. You can use the outside of your hand used for strumming to help with this process. As you stop all the strings, you will mute the guitar rather quickly. Many times, the karate chop is used for a quick stop in the song or at the end of a song. Dramatic moments can also help stop your strings to perfection. However, do not press the strings hard enough that they touch the fretboard and make an unusual sound. You are looking for pure silence here. Lastly, while doing this technique, keep your body still to extenuate the movement.

#6 – A Faded Mute

When it comes to fading, it is completely different from the karate chop. Here is why: the strumming hand gets to sit on the guitar bridge. After you move the mute forward, you will receive a smooth mute that lowers the volume of sound. Think of this as a decrescendo. Also, with individual fingers, you can create a fading mute that helps people who are looking to improvise on their guitar. Sad songs usually have a fading mute more often than not. Some songs are also blues-oriented that finish softly and with finality.

#7 – Using A Pizzicato

The last kind of mute involves the pizzicato, or what is also called the "muted bass." As you play using your thumb, you can rest your entire hand on the bridge of your guitar. This technique kind of sounds like a bass guitar, even if you are playing an electric or acoustic guitar. If you are using a fade mute before a pizzicato, they pair nicely together like peanut butter and jelly.

To make a perfect pizzicato, use a chop down motion on the bridge with your right hand, which is propelled right under the strings. As you roll over the strings with your hand, make sure you go up toward the guitar head for the best pizzicato mute around. With the help of the side of your hand, you can cover the strings and move forward by playing with your thumb. Now that you know the types of mutes, let us talk about when you should use them in the guitar world.

Do Not Sweat the Technique

Using the right muting technique depends on a couple of factors. First, you have to use a mute that you feel most comfortable about. In life, there are times when you are more comfortable with something. For example, when I perform, I believe I can handle myself on guitar and piano, but the guitar is definitely where I feel the most comfortable when I play. Even if a different mute should be used, only use the one that you feel best about.

Normally, when it comes to guitar, the harsher techniques for muting are best for the end of songs. You can make a dramatic moment reality with the right mute. But, if you are muting between notes, go with a mute that is smoother and easier to transition through. Without a chopping motion, you won't make awkward moments in the middle of your song.

Generally speaking, it can be difficult to put muting sounds together and have success. Muting takes time and asks you to practice to make perfect. Even the mood of the people you are playing for shifts what kind of mutes are better than the rest. But, all mutes have their place. It is your job to maneuver the muting world for the best results.

Luckily for you, the techniques you see here are ones that beginners can certainly handle. With the help of tools like this, you can add flavor to the rest of your guitar skills. Even in only a few hours, you will be well on your way to getting all 7 mutes down. Give your music that added layer of beauty, and see how much you improve in the process. Now that you know where to use it, let us talk about the perfect areas in song to drop a mute.

Rest Notes: Rest notes are in songs to add breaks and bring about rest from the musician. Rests are also present, so they stand out when you play. With this in mind, remind yourself of the kinds of rests there are. Remember that for shorter rests, it would be in your best interest to use a muting technique that does not stand out too much. On the other hand, longer rests need that focus and attention, so pick a blatant muting technique here.

Improvisation: An improvisation is a great place for mutes. Every type of musical genre can use a mute, so you can flourish. To get your attention, or those around you, go for a mute that is brash and powerful.

Forgetfulness: No matter what kind of guitarist you are, there will come a time when you will have what the world calls a "brain-fart." You may forget to play something or play a wrong note. A mute is a good trick to fix the problem before things get out a hand. This will allow others to not notice your mistake, and you can move forward with what melody or chord is next.

Practice Agenda

As you get down to practicing, there a few things you need to keep on the forefront of your mind. First, it is in your best interest to come up with a consistent plan on what days and times you are going to rehearse on the guitar. When it comes to this schedule, think about days that are normally free. If you can create a schedule that you can stick to week after week, consistency will pay huge dividends for you, as you look to improve your guitar skill. Muscle memory and building callouses are no joke, so keep working to become the most consistent guitarist around.

Having goals in mind is something you should think through as well. For example, a goal is something obtainable and realistic, but also time-bound. If you want to learn a song 2 years from now, you are probably not going to put in a lot of effort between now and then to reach it. However, if you say you will complete the song in a couple of weeks, a month, or two months, you have to make considerable choices for this to work out. Even within a song, you can say this week that you are going to learn the chorus. The next week, you can learn all the verses, and then onto the bridge following that. It is steps like this that will make practice fun and focused. The more structured you are in the process, the better off you will be down the road.

When thinking about your practice scenario, think about a few starter points. First, find an area where you will not bother someone else and they will not bother you. If you are in your living room, but a family member is watching television there as well, you will both get distracted by the other one. Find a space that will let you focus. Practicing guitar is kind of like studying for an exam or prepping for a speech. That quiet time is essential.

Also, when you are in a quiet place, you will be able to hear what you are doing well and what you are not when playing the guitar. So, find an area for you to gain success. When you can focus in a quiet place, rather than a public place, you will get to pinpoint your areas of need a lot quicker.

Lastly, as you work towards practicing, consider talking with other great guitarists. Senior guitarists are definitively the best above the rest, especially if they are willing to share tips and secrets to the youngsters. If possible, watch them play or join in with them. As you watch and learn, especially with finger movement, you will be able to master a few songs in no time at all. Now, let us move onto some of the most common guitar mistakes.

Chapter 8 – Fixing Beginner Problems

As you continue to become the best beginning guitarist on the planet, there are a variety of common mistakes that you will have to overcome. These problems can come in many forms. But, today, we are going to highlight the most important ones that you should keep an eye on, so you do not make these habitual errors moving forward.

When you are proactive about problems, you may even enjoy the struggle. This might sound outlandish, but it is true. You might want to play guitar even more in hopes that you can conqueror any error on the planet. As stated earlier, the less you challenge yourself, the less you will improve in the long run.

Finger Pain

To start things off, finger pain is an area where guitarists had problems upfront and now it is wreaking havoc on the world around them. Most beginners do not understand the intensity of what they will go through when they play guitar over and over again. Because of this, your fingers will start to cry out immediately or days to follow after you first start playing.

Fortunately for you, there are a few things that you can do to help you onto the road towards healing. First, you may be experiencing pain because of "over-lotioned" hands. You will not have problems with finger pain if your hands are at a somewhat dried-tendency before every guitar session. Ultimately, if your hands are too moisturized, your skin may start to tear and bleed.

Another thing you can do is work with gauged strings. We have talked about this earlier, but you will not have issues with friction when you do this as a beginner. Unfortunately, if you do go for gauged technology, you will lose sound quality in the process. So, you have to weigh the pros and cons here.

Tuning Trouble

Not tuning enough can be a real "Debbie-Downer" for beginner guitarists looking for success. Unfortunately, a lot of beginning guitarists start playing right away without tuning. On your own, this may not be a big deal, but this becomes a major issue when you are playing with other people. Ultimately, the more you play, the more you will know when your guitar is in tune and when it is not. So, trust your inhibitions. You may not be able to gauge tuning from the beginning. However, it should be on your radar at all times.

Sure, this process may be overall tedious, but this should be on your checklist of things to do whenever you look to play the guitar. Remember, some guitars go out of tune quite often. In this instance, you may have to tune the guitar between every song, just so you are on cue.

Being Too Comfortable

Can you be too comfortable when playing the guitar? Yes! You will find what you like and stick with it. This can be a dangerous road because then you get stuck with the same old guitar songs and progressions. There will be no improvement or success stories moving forward because, in your mind, there is no need to stretch yourself. Please do not be this person. These people are weak and bring little to the guitar world.

So you are not extra comfortable, think back to the goals that you want to achieve when playing the guitar. Always have a song that is in your mind next. Look for ways to challenge yourself. Maybe you have just learned the song "Wonderwall." Next, go for the country song "God Gave Me You." Varying your styles and music types will make you an ultimate success story.

Going Too Fast

Earlier in the text, we talked about jumping into a fast song without working your way up can be detrimental for a beginning guitarist. Instead of using repetition to your advantage, you may just move on when you feel that you are ready. This could not be further from the truth about what you should do. Being well rounded is a great quality to have, instead of playing a song so-so during the process. Half-learned songs really will not impress you or your friends.

A lot of times, as guitarists, we think we need to perfect the most difficult parts of a song. While this is a true statement, guitarists also have to not sweat the small stuff either. You will impede your progress, which will limit your guitar playing for the rest of your life if you forget the small things. Hopefully, your passion for guitar will shine here and you will work harder than you ever thought possible towards success.

Playing Too Rough

Beginners can be hard on a guitar. Regrettably, the guitar is usually the one that takes the brunt of the damage. The pick may scratch up the body of the guitar, or the strings may start to wear down as well as the fretboard. You do not have to be Captain America when playing the guitar at the beginning. Think soft and play soft on your wonderful instrument. You will want to keep your guitar around for years to come.

When you start playing for the first time, your hands may be sore and calloused. But, after a few months, you should not be dealing with pain at all. So, do not strum violently and do not press too hard on the strings via the fretboard either. Remember that the cleaner sound will come from you pressing softly and using mutes to extenuate the sound. In the end, take a breath and let the world of guitar relieve your stress and not build upon it.

Forgetting the Metronome

Another common mistake comes in the form of not using the metronome. Especially when you are learning songs for the very first time, the need for a metronome is imperative for achievement. Even in this day and age, professionals use a metronome to keep them on the right path. With a metronome, you may have trouble staying on beat. When this happens, you will be all over the place on a song.

By using a metronome to better orientate yourself, you will be able to play a song just like the original. Speaking of original, another metronome of sorts is the one where you watch a video of the song and try to play along with it. The song from your favorite band will not get offbeat, so why should you?

Bad Positioning

This may be surprising to you, but even a lot of well-versed guitarists do not know how to hold a guitar as they should. Is that not crazy or what? Remember, not holding the guitar correctly does not affect the sound. But, it will affect how your body feels down the line. Remember that your fingers, hands, wrist, arms, shoulders, back, and neck can all be impacted if you have bad habits. If you are still having a problem with this, talk to another guitarist and have them watch your technique. They can help you with some pointers. Some of the best pointers I have ever received came from other guitarists with more wisdom and experience than me.

Poor Fret Pressing

Many mistakes come in the form of pressing frets than in between them. When you press precisely on a fret, you will get a sound that you are not looking for. You may even get a weird muted sound. But, when you play in between the frets, you will have success when playing the right notes and chords.

Lacking Consistency

As stated with practice and preparation, you have to be consistent when playing guitar. Whatever hobby or skill you are trying to learn involves hard-work and consistency. With that in mind, keep up playing a few minutes a day if that is all you can do. The muscle memory will be an important key for your guitar future. Also, try playing guitar right before bed. There is research out there that points to better retention of the instrument at this time of the day.

Chapter 9 – How to Move from A Beginner to An Intermediate Guitar Player

Now that we are wrapping up your beginner guitar experience, remember that there is a lot of room to grow as a musician. To make yourself better and better, hop into more challenging scales and chords. This will put you on the road to intermediate guitar. On top of this, here are some other key ways to become an intermediate guitar player that only you can be.

Playing in The Shadows: When you do shadow playing, it is like you are a boxer in the ring. This process is kind of like air guitar, but you are putting your fingers in their appropriate place. Then, you pretend you are playing the song to the best of your ability. This is one of the best ways to build up the right muscle memory.

Getting Confident: To gain more confidence when playing guitar, challenge yourself, but know when you need to back off as well. You may be pushing yourself on a challenging song. Let us say in this instance, it is too difficult and you are getting frustrated. Stop working on the difficult song for now, and go back to a song that you enjoy. When you have built up confidence again, go back to the challenging song now that you are refreshed and ready to go.

Play with Others: Nothing is more valuable than playing with others around you. This is a very intermediate thing to do. Jamming together brings about creativity. While playing with others, you all will grow by calling out each other's' mistakes and building each other up with encouragement. This is when the guitar gets fun.

Mimic Your Musician Heroes: No matter what kind of guitar you are playing on, watch other musicians that play the same instrument. What kind of techniques do they use? How do they practice? What makes them so passionate about music? Watch videos and grow your knowledge of the craft just like the pros.

Jam More by Yourself: Of course, you should be jamming on your own in general. But, you should be recording yourself every so often, too. This way, you can see how far you have come. Also, you can see how far you still have to go. Improvisation can be done here, as well. Maybe you have been writing your music to this point, and you do not want to forget what you have been working on. This is where recording is essential for growth and development.

Listening to Guitar Music

When you do not have time to play guitar, why not listen to it as much as you can? Maybe you do not have time to play guitar; then, it is a perfect time to put on some tunes that you would like to learn someday or are currently trying to learn. By listening to better guitar influences, you will continue to grow your skill, even if you do not have the time to play.

Chapter 10 – Added Help with Videos & Extra Resources

As we come to the last chapter of the text, I want to leave you with some resources that you can be proud to use. If you are running short on time, check these things out to help teach you new things on the guitar. Hopefully, these resources will add passion and fervor to your guitar playing.

The Gieson Online Guitar Tuner: Maybe you are out and about without a tuner. If you have Wi-Fi access, try this on your laptop or phone. This tuner has over 50 types of tunings, which can be fun if you are looking to diversify your growth on the guitar.

Guitar Tab Template: Are you looking to be a master composer someday? Using the Guitar Tab Template can help get you there. On this site, you can make up your tablature, so you can keep it around for years to come. This is great no matter if you are a beginner or an expert in the field of the guitar.

GuitarJamz: If you are a big fan of watching videos on YouTube about guitar, get yourself familiarized with GuitarJamz. It is purely the YouTube of guitars. They have lessons to help you at your own pace. This site is like you are at guitar school, but you do not have to pay a dime of your money. All you need is Internet access to make it happen. With videos for beginners up to experts, this resource is for you.

Ultimate Guitar Tabs: We talked about this resource earlier, but it is worth conversation again. This site has the most tablature on planet Earth. And remember that all this stuff is free, free, and free. From the most popular songs to the most obscure, you can find everything you need here. For the catchiest of songs, check out Ultimate Guitar Tabs for all your tablature needs. Lastly, Guitar Tab Template is run by Ultimate Guitar Tabs, so it is like you get two for one here.

Jamplay.com: If you are looking for another resource to help you that is similar to YouTube, then check out Jamplay.com. It is a little different from GuitarJamz. The lessons go a lot faster and they may seem a little frenzied. But, the site wants you to learn in different ways like you never have before. With the help of professional guitars, you will love the way this site helps guitarists all over the world.

For more great information, check out the resources page at the end of the book. There are so many more sites and options for you to consider there. We have just scratched the surface here. So, you may want to skip the conclusion if you are looking for more things to make practice rock.

Conclusion

Well, we have come to the end. I hope you have learned something in this book that will propel you into a love for guitar. And, over the next 7 days, I expect great things from you as you learn your first song. We have covered so many topics in this book, but let us walk through all you should have learned, shall we? Check out the list below:

- Guitar Parts
- The Different Types of Guitars
- Stringing Guitars
- Holding A Guitar
- Playing with Both Hands
- Techniques for Tuning
- Naming the Guitar Strings
- Playing Guitar Notes
- Reading Sheet Music and Tablature
- Working on Three Notes
- Knowing Major and Minor Chords
- All the Ways to Mute
- Beginner Mistakes
- Guitar Improvements
- Further Resources

It is truly amazing how much stuff you went through. You should be proud of the places you went to and where you are heading now. So, be consistent and go and rock the world of guitar. Know that it will not be easy. But, with focus and determination, you can learn the guitar, no matter what age you find yourself. But, if there is one thing that I would leave you with, it should be to have fun. The guitar was meant for the passionate and the joyful, so live that life. Good luck with playing the guitar!

Resources Page

Andrews, Dan. (2011). *Learn to Play the Guitar in 10 Hours – No Musical Talent Required*. Retrieved from https://www.tropicalmba.com/learn-to-play-guitar/.

Bateman, Lauren. (n.d.). *Guitar Lesson Articles & Tips*. Retrieved from https://www.laurenbateman.com/guitar-lesson-articles.

Duffy, T. (2019). *How to Get Started Playing Guitar: 10 Beginner FAQs*. Retrieved from https://www.fender.com/articles/how-to/for-those-about-to-rock-10-beginner-faqs.

Ferrante, D. (2017). *Guitar book for adult beginners: teach yourself how to play famous guitar songs, guitar chords, theory & technique*. United States: Steeplechase Arts.

Guitar Jamz. (2018). Retrieved from https://guitarjamz.com/premium/.

Guitar World Staff. (2015). *New Study Shows How Guitar Players' Brains Are Different from Everybody Else's*. Retrieved from https://www.guitarworld.com/features/new-study-shows-how-guitar-players-brains-are-different-everybody-elses.

Jamplay.com (2020). *JamPlay*, Retrieved from www.jamplay.com.

Music Radar (n.d.). *Music tuition*. Retrieved from https://www.musicradar.com/tuition.

Online Guitar Tuner. (2020). Retrieved from https://www.gieson.com/Library/projects/utilities/tuner/.

The Guardian. (2020). *Learn to play guitar*. Retrieved from https://www.theguardian.com/lifeandstyle/2014/mar/22/how-to-learn-play-guitar.

The Guitar Lesson. (2019). *Best Way Teach Yourself Guitar*. Retrieved from https://www.theguitarlesson.com/articles/teach-yourself-guitar/.

Stewart, T. (2019). *Online Guitar Lessons / Learn Guitar with HD Video Lessons*. Retrieved from www.jamplay.com.

Ultimate Guitar. (2020). Retrieved from www.ultimate-guitar.com.

Vasister, Neelesh. (2014). Learn Guitar Chords – A Guide for Beginners. Retrieved from https://www.uberchord.com/blog/learn-guitar-chords/.

YouTube. (2020). Retrieved from www.youtube.com.

www.ingramcontent.com/pod-product-compliance
Lightning Source LLC
Chambersburg PA
CBHW081158070526
44583CB00021B/2904